☆☆☆☆☆☆☆☆☆☆☆☆☆☆☆☆

# 888

## Reasons to Hate

# REPUBLICANS

☆☆☆☆☆☆☆☆☆☆☆☆☆☆☆☆☆☆☆☆☆

☆☆☆☆☆☆☆☆☆☆☆☆☆☆☆☆☆☆☆☆☆☆☆☆☆

# 888

## Reasons to Hate
# REPUBLICANS

An A to Z Guide to Everything Loathsome
About the Party of the Arrogant Rich

**BARBARA LAGOWSKI AND RICK MUMMA**

A BIRCH LANE PRESS BOOK
Published by Carol Publishing Group

☆☆☆☆☆☆☆☆☆☆☆☆☆☆☆☆☆☆☆☆☆☆☆☆☆

A Birch Lane Press Book
Published by Carol Publishing Group
Birch Lane Press is a registered trademark of Carol Communications, Inc.
Editorial, sales and distribution, rights and permissions inquiries should be addressed to
Carol Publishing Group, 120 Enterprise Avenue, Secaucus, NJ 07094.

In Canada: Canadian Manda Group, One Atlantic Avenue, Suite 105, Toronto, Ontario
    M6K 3E7

Carol Publishing Books may be purchased in bulk at special discounts for sales promotion,
fund-raising, or educational purposes. Special editions can be created to specifications. For
details, contact: Special Sales Department, Carol Publishing Group, 120 Enterprise Avenue,
Secaucus, NJ 07094.

Manufactured in the United States of America
10 9 8 7 6 5 4 3 2 1

Library of Congress Cataloging-in-Publication Data

Lagowski, Barbara.
    888 reasons to hate Republicans : an A to Z guide to everything loathsome about the
party of the arrogant rich / Barbara Lagowski and Rick Mumma.
        p. cm.
    "A Birch Lane Press book."
    ISBN 1-55972-370-X (pb)
    1. United States—Politics and government—1993 —Humor.
2. Republican Party (U.S. : 1854– )—Humor.    I Mumma, Rick.
II. Title.
E885.L345   1996                                              96-34152
324.2734'0207—dc20                                           CIP

They don't respond to the announcement "Blue Light Special"
Their boxes of "flesh-toned" Crayolas contain one crayon.
But are there really
*888 Reasons to Hate Republicans?*

You bet your irrevocable trust fund dividend there are! And this politically incorrect litany of memorable party lines ("I am not a crook"), symbols, and slurs resurrects them all just in time for what promises to be another mud-slinging, mind-numbing election season.

Remember George Bush's benevolent nod to the "little brown ones"? The partywide misconception that the boat people were victims of a badly-run regatta? We do. And in this non-federally funded (and therefore completed in our lifetimes) collection of Grand Old political foibles past and present, we reveal more Republican quirks and curiosities than there are ways to spell "potatoe." Including, what Republicans believe (*"The only electrically powered vehicle they believe in is the one that transports them from the first tee to*

*the 'nineteenth hole'"); their strengths (*"Their family jewels are actually jewels"*); and, of course, their weaknesses (*"They can't bowl worth a damn"*).

Of course, there are many ugly commonalities that Republicans and Democrats share. Like law degrees. Embarrassing relatives. And Martha Stewart. But their most memorable characteristics are like Fawn Hall—clearly split along party lines.

Written in brief, biting, out-of-context and *always* negative sound bites (just like your favorite news broadcast!), a book that is sure to give Mrs. Gingrich something else to bitch about, this collection is our paean to the political party whose dogs write books, who instinctively aim twenty-one-gun salutes toward Moscow, and who believe in a thousand points of light . . . and enough live-in help to turn them all on.

☆☆☆☆☆☆☆☆☆☆☆☆☆☆☆☆☆☆☆☆☆☆☆☆

Politics . . . the systematic organization of hatreds.
—Henry Adams, *The Education of Henry Adams*

Hell, I never vote *for* anybody, I always vote *against.*
—W. C. Fields

☆☆☆☆☆☆☆☆☆☆☆☆☆☆☆☆☆☆☆☆☆☆☆☆☆

# 888

## Reasons to Hate
# REPUBLICANS

☆☆☆☆☆☆☆☆☆☆☆☆☆☆☆☆☆☆☆☆☆☆☆☆☆

☆☆☆☆☆☆☆☆☆☆☆☆☆☆☆☆☆☆☆☆☆☆☆☆

1.    Abstinence is their preferred method of birth control.

2.    They would rather outfit the family in acid rain-proof
      L.L Bean "barn coats" than place intrusive regulations
      on the smokestacks of America..

3.    They prefer acquisitiveness to inquisitiveness.

4.    Spiro Agnew, "a flat-out knee-crawling slug with the
      morals of a weasel on speed." —Hunter Thompson

5.    Airline deregulation (now instead of flying for peanuts,
      they're what we get for lunch)

6. Lamar Alexander's red lumberjack shirt

7. They prefer the Second Amendment to the Fifth.

8. After they amend the bill of rights to allow school prayer, they're going to edit that ridiculous "camel through the needle's eye" metaphor right out of the Gospel of Matthew.

9. The American Bar Association

10. American "cheese"

11. They don't see the irony in the painting *American Gothic.*

12. The American Legion

13. The American Medical Association

14. *American Spectator*

15. Americans who yell, "USA . . . USA!" while the Olympic basketball "Dream Team" is elbowing its way to a 127-2 victory over the Armenians

16. Ample waistlines

17. Animal experimentation

18. Anita Bryant

19. They read annual reports for pleasure

20. Antisodomy laws

21. They never go anywhere without an appointment calendar.

22. Arbitrageurs

23. They can tell you what an arbitrageur does to earn his eight-figure salary.

24. Argyle

25. Representative Dick Armey

26. Arizona

27. They look forward to Armageddon as "that big A-list soiree in the sky."

28. Laura Ashley prints

29. Assault weapons

30. They secretly used White House astrologers to time everything from the delivery of new china to new China policies.

31. Attica is their model for prison reform.

32. *Au pairs*

33. They would give more autonomy to the states, including the likes of Mississippi, Alabama, and Utah.

34. Jim and Tammy Bakker

35. They use bald eagles in interior decoration.

36. They use bald eagles in exterior decoration.

37. Bald eagle hunters and their inalienable right to bear arms and protect their private property from unauthorized overflight

★☆☆☆☆☆☆☆☆☆☆☆☆☆☆☆☆☆☆☆☆

38. Banks

39. Bankers

40. Barcaloungers

41. They think the only time "Black is Beautiful" is in their accounting ledger.

42. Bean counters

43. They became alarmed when Ray Charles sang "America the Beautiful."

44. They became apoplectic when Jimi Hendrix mangled the "Star Spangled Banner."

45. They're suspicious of what might be hiding "behind every bush," but wouldn't think of picking up a hedge clipper to check.

46. They believe that charity should begin (and end) at home.

47. *The Bell Curve*

48. They confuse the fictional plight of a TV character played by Candace Bergen with the real problems of unwed mothers.

49. Bermuda

50. Bermuda shorts

51.   Beverly Hills

52.   The Bible Belt

53.   Bible thumping

54.   Big business

55.   Big Men on Campus

56.   The Big Tent theory of party membership, embracing a
      wide range of Republican opinion from conservative
      crackpots like Pat Buchanan to conservative crackpots
      like the Michigan militia

57. They're against bilingual education unless *la deuxième langue* is being taught at a pricey private Lycée.

58. Billionaires who fly coach, drive their own pickup trucks, get cheap haircuts, and refuse to surgically alter their ears to prove they're just like you and me

59. Billions in federal handouts spent on Newt Gingrich's middle-class congressional district

60. The John Birch Society

61. Ollie North's birthday cake for the Ayatollah

62. The Pentagon's sacrosanct black budget

☆ ☆ ☆ ☆ ☆ ☆ ☆ ☆ ☆ ☆ ☆ ☆ ☆ ☆ ☆ ☆ ☆ ☆ ☆ ☆ ☆

63. They blackball country club applicants who are not "our kind of people."

64. Blacklists

65. Bland ingredients

66. Blind obedience

67. "Republicans are . . . bloodsuckers with offices in Wall Street, princes of privilege, plunderers." —Harry S. Truman giving 'em hell in 1948

68. Bluebloods

69. Blood lines

70.

71. Boards of Directors

72. The Bohemian Grove

73. Bomb Shelters

74. They spend billions on batwinged B-2 bombers but grouse about the cost of school lunches.

75. "I've signed legislation that will outlaw Russia forever. We begin bombing in five minutes." —Ronald Reagan

76. Congressman Salvatore "Sonny" Bono—at least he's more convincing in has role as a reactionary representative than he was as a Hollywood hippie.

77. Pat Boone

78. Bootcamps for juvenile offenders

79. Bootcamps for everyone whose father wasn't powerful enough to get them into the National Guard

80. Fondness for bootstrap and grindstone metaphors

81. They're boring.

82. Robert Bork's beard (the real source of the infamous "pubic hair" on Clarence Thomas's Coke can)

83. They're born with a "silver foot" in their mouths.

84. Boston Brahmins

85. They do not consider "bourgeois" an epithet.

86. They learn to tie a bow tie before they learn to tie their shoes.

87. Bread lines

88. Bridge

89. Brooks Brothers

☆☆☆☆☆☆☆☆☆☆☆☆☆☆☆☆☆☆☆☆☆☆☆☆

90. Floyd Brown, creator of the Willie Horton commercials and distributor of free Gennifer Flowers tapes

91. Pat Buchanan

92. William F. Buckley

93. Budget impasses

94. Buick Roadmasters

95. They think Archie Bunker was too lenient with "Meathead."

96. Burberry raincoats

97. Burberry raincoats on Springer spaniels

98. Burghers

99. They would protect book burning and witch burning before flag burning.

100. Frank Burns

101. Montgomery Burns

102. George Bush's unconventional method of "passing the sushi" to the Prime Minister of Japan

103. Business Class

☆ ☆ ☆ ☆ ☆ ☆ ☆ ☆ ☆ ☆ ☆ ☆ ☆ ☆ ☆ ☆ ☆ ☆ ☆ ☆ ☆ ☆ ☆

104. Business majors

105. "The business of America is business." —Calvin Coolidge

106. "The business of government is to keep the government out of business—that is, unless business needs government aid." —Will Rogers

107. Butlers

108. Buttoned-down minds

109. Buttoned-down Oxford shirts

110. Buttoned-up overcoats

111. Earl Butz's stand-up routines on those ethnic differences we all find so hilarious

112. Cabin cruisers

113. They believe that Star Wars is a viable defense strategy, but can't believe that George McGovern flew 35 successful missions as a bomber pilot in World War II.

114. Campaign promises

115. The Canon of Dead White Males

116. They can't bowl worth a damn.

117. Capital gains tax cuts were the only issue that George Bush understood on a gut level.

☆ ☆ ☆ ☆ ☆ ☆ ☆ ☆ ☆ ☆ ☆ ☆ ☆ ☆ ☆ ☆ ☆ ☆ ☆ ☆ ☆ ☆ ☆ ☆

118. "Capitalist pornography" (any book by or about Donald Trump, H. Ross Perot, Warren Buffett, Bill Gates, et al.)

119. Captains of industry

120. Car phones

121. Car radios preset to easy listening stations

122. They have "careers" rather than lives.

123. Cashmere sweater sets

124. *Caveat emptor n* [Lat.] (1523): let the seller make profits unimpeded by consumer "rights" legislation

125. When they hear "CD," they think of fat Cerificates of Deposit, not Hootie and the Blowfish.

126. People who use cellular phones in public

127. They want to censor everything but the *700 Club* and Newt's mother.

128. CEOs

129. CFOs

130. COOs

131. Chanel No. 5

132. Charity galas in which the charity is only an excuse for getting the good jewelry out of the vault

133. Chase Manhattan

134. "Every Republican candidate for President since 1936 has been nominated by the Chase National Bank."
—Robert A. Taft

135. Chauvinism

136. Checkers (the dog, not the game)

137. They believe that when Christ comes back he'll be a social conservative with a trickle-down strategy for salvation.

138. The Christian Coalition

139. CIA

140. Gas-guzzling Cigarette-brand speedboats

141. Cigar aficionados (the real reason Republicans are still pissed off at Fidel after more than 35 years in power)

142. Tom Clancy

143. The myth of a classless America perpetrated by members of private clubs living off dividends

144. Club ties

☆ ☆ ☆ ☆ ☆ ☆ ☆ ☆ ☆ ☆ ☆ ☆ ☆ ☆ ☆ ☆ ☆ ☆ ☆ ☆ ☆

145. They don't mind if a few baby seals are clubbed in order to buy their wives fur coats.

146. They coach Little League teams to win at all costs.

147. Coach™ handbags

148. Coffee houses that serve up $5.50 cappuccinos to businessmen rather than culture and poetry

149. The Cold War

150. Colt .45 (the firearm, not the beverage)

151. They waste great coming-out parties on people who will never leave the closet.

152. People who are called "Commodore" of a lakefront yacht club

153. Commuters

154. Compassion fatigue

155. The Competitive Enterprise Institute

156. They complain about the dark side of television, then treat us all to a televised journey up their colons.

157. "If people demonstrate in a manner to interfere with others, they should be rounded up and put in concentration camps." —Ex-Attorney General Richard Kleindienst

☆☆☆☆☆☆☆☆☆☆☆☆☆☆☆☆☆☆☆☆☆☆☆☆

158. They fly on the Concorde.

159. Condos overlooking the eighteenth fairway

160. Conformity

161. They tend to confuse the accident of fortunate birth
with virtue or hard work.

162. Conglomerates

163. Congressional perks

164. Congressional junkets

165. Fairfield, Connecticut

166. "A Conservative is a man with two perfectly good legs who, however, has never learned to walk forward. A Reactionary is a somnambulist walking backward."
—Franklin D. Roosevelt

167. "Conservatives are not necessarily stupid, but most stupid people are conservatives." —John Stuart Mill

168. They consider any movie involving assault weapons a "nightmare of depravity". . . unless it stars Arnold Schwarzenegger or anyone else on the GOP donors list.

169. Conspiracy nuts

170. "Constructive engagement" with apartheid South Africa

☆☆☆☆☆☆☆☆☆☆☆☆☆☆☆☆☆☆☆☆☆☆☆

171. Newt Gingrich's Contract with America

172. Newt Gingrich's Contract with the American Family

173. Newt Gingrich's contract with HarperCollins

174. Calvin Coolidge

175. Corporate American Express gold cards

176. Corporate jets

177. Corporate lawyers

178. Cost-benefit analyses

179. Country clubs

180. Country Day Schools

181. Country decorating as exemplified by folk art stools with udders and teats

182. George Bush's country-music-and-pork-rinds act

183. Country Squires

184. Country Squire station wagons

185. They only get cozy with Communists when it's in the interest of American businesses looking for large, untapped markets and sources of cheap labor.

☆☆☆☆☆☆☆☆☆☆☆☆☆☆☆☆☆☆☆☆☆☆☆☆

186. CPAs

187. Creationism

188. Their credit cards are never rejected in full view of everybody else in the Wal-Mart checkout line.

189. They think crew is a great preparation for Republicanism because it trains young men to sit down and go backward.

190. Betty Crocker

191. "I am not a crook." —Richard Milhous Nixon

192. "When the president does it, that means it is not illegal." —Richard Milhous Nixon

☆☆☆☆☆☆☆☆☆☆☆☆☆☆☆☆☆☆☆☆☆☆☆

193. Cruises

194. They still use cufflinks.

195. The "Cultural Civil War"

196. Currency speculators

197. They want to avenge Custer's Last Stand.

198. Dallas

199. Dynasty

200. The Dallas Cowboys

☆☆☆☆☆☆☆☆☆☆☆☆☆☆☆☆☆☆☆☆☆☆☆

201. The Daughters of the American Revolution

202. The daughters of Richard Nixon

203. They are disturbed that Sammy Davis, Jr. kissed Richard Nixon with more emotion than was ever shown by Pat.

204. Doris Day

205. Deficit spending

206. They defined anti-war protesters as rioters.

207. They defined the Contras as "the moral equivalent to our Founding Fathers."

208. They define freedom of expression as the constitutional right of vinyl siding telemarketers to call your home phone number at any time of the day or night (but preferably during dinner).

209. Reagan "Democrats"

210. Southern "Democrats"

211. They understood this "depreciation" tax scam.

212. The Depression

213. They deregulate cable prices and regulate cable content.

214. They prefer a Cadillac Fleetwood to Fleetwood Mac.

215. The Dirty Tricks unit of the committee to re-elect Tricky Dick

216. Disciplinarians

217. They support the Disneyfication of American culture.

218. Dittoheads who admit that Rush does all their thinking for them

219. They do not react to the announcement, "Blue-light special."

220. They care more about their dogs than they do the homeless.

221. Dog-eat-dog competition

222. They prefer dogs to cats because they value blind obedience.

223. "[George Bush] has the look about him of someone who might sit up and yip for a dog yummie." —Mike Royko, columnist

224. They own dogs that "write" books.

225. "I'm willing to be another Ronald Reagan if that's what you want." —Bob Dole

226. They don't find it the least bit ironic that Ronald Reagan was the host of TV's *Death Valley Days*.

☆ ☆ ☆ ☆ ☆ ☆ ☆ ☆ ☆ ☆ ☆ ☆ ☆ ☆ ☆ ☆ ☆ ☆ ☆ ☆ ☆ ☆ ☆

227. Dom Perignon

228. Bob Dornan

229. Morton Downey Jr., who blazed a broadcasting trail so wide that even someone as fat as Rush Limbaugh could follow

230. They drape themselves in the flag even though those colors do not flatter anyone's skin tones.

231. Dress codes

232. Dressage

233. Dressing for dinner

234. Dressing for success

☆ ☆ ☆ ☆ ☆ ☆ ☆ ☆ ☆ ☆ ☆ ☆ ☆ ☆ ☆ ☆ ☆ ☆ ☆ ☆ ☆

235. Dressing for bed

236. Ducks as decorating accents, or, even worse, phones

237. David Duke

238. Phyllis Schlafly's *Eagle Forum*

239. Eagle scouts

240. Efficiency experts

241. The eighteen minutes of silence on tape

242. One minute of government-mandated silence in class-rooms

243. The only electrically-powered vehicle they believe in is the one that transports them from the first tee to the "nineteenth hole."

244. Elephants draped in festive red, white, and blue buntings—or, in Barbara Bush's case, just blue

245. Elitism

246. The Elks Club

247. Emotional restraint

248. Empower America

249. Empty Suits

250. The endearing grandfatherly senility of Ronald Wilson Reagan

251. Enemies Lists

252. The fact that I was left off of Nixon's Enemies List

253. English First

254. Entrepreneurs

255. Their idea of environmental laws are local ordinances governing the legal height of grass on residential lawns.

256. Epidemic affluenza

☆ ☆ ☆ ☆ ☆ ☆ ☆ ☆ ☆ ☆ ☆ ☆ ☆ ☆ ☆ ☆ ☆ ☆ ☆ ☆ ☆ ☆ ☆

257. Episcopalians

258. They killed the Equal Rights Amendment

259. The Establishment

260. Ethan Allen furniture

261. Ethnocentrism

262. Executive bonuses

263. "Executive homes"

264. Executive privilege

265. Expense accounts

266. Expense account lunches

267. Expletives deleted

268. Exxon

269. They have faith in the justice system only when the jury is picked in Simi Valley.

270. Fake convertible tops on large American cars

271. Jerry Falwell

272. The Family Cap (the Congressional version of China's one-child policy)

273. Their family jewels are actually jewels.

274. Their family values are actually valuables

275. The fat forgotten Presidents: William Howard Taft, Rutherford B. Hayes, and Chester A. Arthur

276. The fatness of Rush Limbaugh

277. The FBI

278. Fifteen-second attack ads

279. "A conservative is a man too cowardly to fight and too fat to run." —Elbert Hubbard

280. Filibusters against civil rights legislation

281. Filofaxes

282. They are dissappointed that *Firing Line* doesn't involve the use of rifles and live ammunition on liberal guests.

283. They mark time in terms of fiscal years.

284. They only catch fish they can hang on the wall.

285. Five-hundred-dollar-a-plate fund-raisers

286. Flag-factory photo ops

287. Flagrant flag wavers every Fourth of July who would
     have been temperamentally Tories on July 4, 1776

288. Marilyn Quayle's "flip" hairstyle

289. Florsheims

290. Flower shows

291. They fly first class (as long as it's on the company's
     tab).

292. For-profit hospitals

293.

294. Capitalist tool Malcom S. Forbes, Sr.

295. Presidential monkey wrench Malcolm S. Forbes, Jr.

296. Gerald Ford for giving a pardon to Richard Nixon

297. Gerald Ford for giving a career to Chevy Chase

298. They don't trust any foreign government that wasn't installed by the CIA.

299. *Fortune*

300. The great 401K conspiracy to turn otherwise normal people into Republicans by tying all their retirement funds to the fate of the stock market

301. Fox hunts

302. Anyone who dresses like a fox hunter on any day other than Halloween

303. Fraternities

304. Frequent flyer miles for F-16 pilots during the Reagan era

305. They are more frightened by the actions of nine people in black robes in Washington D.C. than by the actions of a mob in white robes in rural Alabama.

306. Frigidity

307. Mark Fuhrman's tape-recorded claim that all his buddies on the L.A.P.D. are Republicans

308. They are proud of the increasing gap between rich and poor.

309. If they don't mind gassing, clubbing, and electrocuting humans, why should we expect them to mind the gassing, clubbing, and electrocution of the original owners of their fur coats?

☆☆☆☆☆☆☆☆☆☆☆☆☆☆☆☆☆☆☆☆☆☆☆

310. Gated communities

311. General Electric

312. General Motors

313. Generals who think they should be President

314. Gentrification

315. The landed gentry

316. They get all those strange growths on their noses but never once think of Pinocchio.

☆☆☆☆☆☆☆☆☆☆☆☆☆☆☆☆☆☆☆☆☆☆☆☆

317. Kathie Lee Gifford

318. Newt Gingrich

319. George Gipp

320. The glass ceiling

321. Go-getters, self-starters, and all the other eager beavers who make life hell for the rest of us

322. Golden parachutes

323. Golden retrievers

☆☆☆☆☆☆☆☆☆☆☆☆☆☆☆☆☆☆☆☆☆☆

324. Their golden rule: He who has the gold makes the rules

325. Barry Goldwater before he was mellowed by senility

326. Golf

327. Golf carts with cellular phones

328. Golf fashions

329. Golf on network television

330. Oversize golf umbrellas on crowded city sidewalks

331. The "good old days"

☆☆☆☆☆☆☆☆☆☆☆☆☆☆☆☆☆☆☆☆☆☆☆☆

332. "Good" wars

333. They get goosebumps at the sound of marching glock-enspiels.

334. GOPAC

335. Government shutdowns

336. "God created Adam and Eve, not Adam and Steve."
—Anita Bryant

337. Goyim

338. Billy Graham

339. Phil Gramm

340. Grand Marnier

341. Congressman Fred "Gopher" Grandy

342. Gray suits

343. Greed

344. The last time they used the term "greenhouse effect" they were talking to an architect and pointing to the south side of the house.

345. Greenwich lockjaw

346. Grenada, Panama, Libya, and Iraq were only skirmishes; the public opinion polls were the real wars.

347. Gridlock

348. Gucci loafers

349. Gucci scarves

350. Gun racks

351. General Alexander "I'm in charge here" Haig

352. The Great Communicator

353. Halcion-induced dementia

354. Haldeman and Erlichman

355. Fawn Hall

356. The Hamptons

357. The New Harshness

358. Them that has, gets

359. "Hate the sin but love the sinner"

360. They have never eaten Jell-O Jigglers.

361. "HAVE YOU SLUGGED YOUR KID TODAY?" —bumper sticker on a car owned by Alfred S. Regnery, Reagan administration nominee for Director of the Office of Juvenile Justice and Delinquency Prevention

362. Hawks

363. Health care reforms that will cover the poor and the elderly . . . with six feet of dirt

364. Heir(esse)s

365. Jesse Helms

366. Leona Helmsley

367. The Heritage Foundation

368. Charlton Heston

369. They own more Holy Bibles than pairs of holey jeans.

370. They don't mind if there are homeless people living in cars as long as they've got enough gas to get out of town.

371. Homogenization

372. Homophobia

373. Herbert Hoover

☆☆☆☆☆☆☆☆☆☆☆☆☆☆☆☆☆☆☆☆☆☆☆

374. J. Edgar Hoover

375. The Hoover Institute

376. Hoovervilles

377. Bob Hope

378. Horse shows

379. They will only support medical reforms that make hospital-bed divorce papers easier to sign.

380. The House Un-American Activities Committee

☆☆☆☆☆☆☆☆☆☆☆☆☆☆☆☆☆☆☆☆☆☆☆

381. Mike and Ariana Huffington

382. Hummel figurines

383. Humorlessness

384.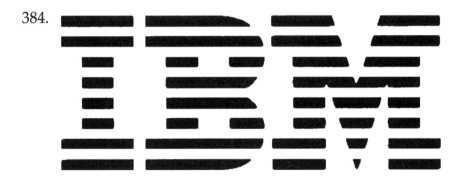

385. They prefer the Ice Capades to ballet.

386. "IF GUNS ARE OUTLAWED, ONLY OUTLAWS WILL HAVE GUNS"
—NRA bumper sticker

387. Sen. Alfonse D'Amato's imitation of Lance Ito

388. Incautious invitations to lip readers

389. Their indiscriminate flag waving

390. They're rich enough to worry about inheritance taxes kicking in after the first six hundred grand.

391. They install expensive basketball hoops in every suburban driveway, but haven't sent one of their own to the NBA since 1957.

392. Insurance companies

393. Pathological interest in interest rate fluctuations

394. Investment bankers

395. Iowa

396. Idaho, the home of the Aryan Nation.

397. Indiana, the birthplace of the Ku Klux Klan and Dan Quayle.

398. Any of those kook-magnet states whose name begins with an "I"

399. They're almost as proud of tearing down the Iron Curtain as they are of building a ten-foot-high steel wall between California and Mexico.

400. "Gourmet" jellybeans

401. Keeping up with the Joneses

402. They *are* the Joneses

403. The Junior League

404. Junk bonds

405. "Just say no"

☆☆☆☆☆☆☆☆☆☆☆☆☆☆☆☆☆☆☆☆☆☆☆

406. Kennebunkport

407. Jack Kemp

408. Kent State

409. They classify ketchup as a vegetable

410. Key Biscayne

411. They know how to do the "Fox Trot."

412. They know the difference between ecru, natural, ivory, oyster, and a dozen other permutations of beige.

413. They know their tax brackets.

☆ ☆ ☆ ☆ ☆ ☆ ☆ ☆ ☆ ☆ ☆ ☆ ☆ ☆ ☆ ☆ ☆ ☆ ☆ ☆ ☆ ☆

414. Krugerrands

415. They lack rhythm on the dance floor and think everyone else should practice it in the bedroom.

416. Ladies who lunch

417. Ladies

418. They would solve the landfill problem by filling the
Grand Canyon with bald tires and poop-filled Huggies.

419. Landlords

420. Laser weapons

421. Cosmetic laser surgery

422. Law and order

423. Lawn Boys

424. La-Z-Boys

425. Leaf blowers

426. Lean and mean workforces cut to the bone for the immediate gratification of fat and lazy stockholders

427. They learned their history from John Wayne movies.

428. Leather briefcases

429. Leather car seats

430. Too much left brain

431. Legacy admissions to Ivy League colleges

432. Want to cut off free legal services for the poor ("Hey, Johnnie Cochran has to earn a living, too.")

433. The leisure class

434. Leisure suits

435. Prefer Leno to Letterman

436. Liberace

437. "The Republican party either corrupts its liberals or it expels them."  —Harry S. Truman

438. "Liberals feel unworthy of their possessions. Conservatives feel they deserve everything they've stolen."  —Mort Sahl

439. G. Gordon Liddy

440. Rush Limbaugh

441. Limousines

☆☆☆☆☆☆☆☆☆☆☆☆☆☆☆☆☆☆☆☆☆☆☆☆

442. The fact that the party of Lincoln is now the party of Lincoln Continentals

443. "If Lincoln were alive today, he'd roll over in his grave." —Gerald Ford

444. "I'm a Ford, not a Lincoln." —Gerald Ford

445. Lions (the organization, not the animals)

446. "Lite" rock

447. Their litmus test on abortion

448. The "little brown ones" (George Bush's half-Hispanic grandchildren)

449. They live in suburbs where they never have to confront their racism.

450. They live in the past.

451. "Most people don't have the luxury of living to be eighty years old so it's kind of hard for me to feel sorry for them." —Phil Gramm

452. Loan officers, and all other gatekeepers of the American Dream.

453. Lockouts

454. Logrolling ("I'll vote for your nuclear power plant if you vote for my golf-course preservation act.")

455. Long Dong Silver

456. They long for Armageddon.

457. They look, without apparent irony, for business advice from Genghis Khan and Attila the Hun.

458. They look out for number one.

459. They prefer Lotus 1-2-3 to the lotus position.

460. Love Canal

461. LOVE IT OR LEAVE IT bumper stickers

462. Loyalty oaths

463. The LPGA

464. Richard Lugar's Howdy Doody smile

465. The lunatic fringe

466. Tax-deductible lunches

467. Lutherans

468. Luxury skyboxes

469. They became the majority party by pandering to the majority race.

470. The Man in the Gray Flannel Suit

471. They think manatees should develop thicker skins, but don't care if Bob Dole ever does.

472. Mandatory attendance at corporate parties, picnics, and golf tournaments

473. Mandatory death sentences

474. Mandatory drug testing

475. Mandatory sentencing

476. They install imposing marble and brass lobbies in corporate headquarters to keep out the riffraff.

477. Marching bands

478. If you mention "the Market" to them, they think of the New York Stock Exchange, not the Piggly Wiggly.

479. They marry women that look like their grandmothers.

480. They marry men that look like good providers.

481. They lived like Martha Stewart before Martha Stewart was born.

482. Martial law

483. Martial music

484. Martinis

485. Three-martini lunches

486. Tax-deductible three-martini lunches

487. Jackie Mason

488. Mary Matalin

489. Their only -ism is materialism.

490. Mayonnaise

491. MBAs

492. McCarthyism

493. Profits for McDonalds, McJobs for the rest of us

494. Medicaid cuts

495. Medicare cuts

496. Ed Meese

497. They meet the finest people  at the Betty Ford clinic.

498. They'd like to add a little bleach to the Melting Pot.

499. Men's loafers with tassels

500. Men's loafers with little kilts

501. Men's loafers with tassels and little kilts

502. Men's loafers with tassels and little kilts and golf spikes

503. Mendacity

504. Merchant bankers

505. Mercury Grand Marquises

506. Mergers and acquisitions

507. The enduring metaphorical paradox of stuffed shirts in empty suits

☆ ☆ ☆ ☆ ☆ ☆ ☆ ☆ ☆ ☆ ☆ ☆ ☆ ☆ ☆ ☆ ☆ ☆ ☆ ☆ ☆ ☆

508. The Michigan Militia

509. Microsoft

510. "Middle-class" millionaires

511. Military-style haircuts

512. The military-industrial complex

513. Military schools

514. Michael Milken

515. Mink ranchers

516. Misogynists

517. *Mister Rogers' Neighborhood*

518. They believe modern art's okay once an artist has shown a proven return on investment.

519. "Moloch whose mind is pure machinery!  Moloch whose blood is running money!"  —Alan Ginsberg, *Howl*

520.

521. Monogrammed cufflinks

522. Monogrammed white shirts

523. Monogrammed leather briefcases

524. Monopolies

525. Monopoly is their favorite game, but you'd better watch them like a hawk when they volunteer to be the banker.

526. Their moral compasses have needles that only point right.

527. The Moral Majority

528. They're more likely to believe God is behind the AIDS plague than the CIA.

529. Mormons

530. "Morning in America"

531. Georgette Mosbacher

532. Movers and shakers

533. Mudslinging

534. Rupert Murdoch

535. Muzak

536. They're mystified by those amazing laser devices that scan grocery prices.

537. They saddle innocent infants with names like Cornelia, Eugenia, and Upshur, but call their fifty-year-old friends Muffy, Biff, and Skip.

538. National Empowerment Television

539. The National Football League

540. The National Rifle Association

541. *The National Review*

542. Nativism

543. Navy blue suits

544. Navy blue blazers with brass buttons and an embroi-
dered nautical motif on the breast pocket

545. Negative campaigning

546. Neo-Victorian domestic architecture, to match their
neo-Victorian social philosophy

547. New Hampshire

548. New money

549. Newport

550. The 1950s

551. Exclusive zip codes like 90210

552. The 1980s

553. 1984 (the election year)

554. *Nineteen Eighty-Four* (the book)

555. The 1992 Republican National Convention

556.

557. "Nobody talks more of free enterprise and competition and of the best man winning than the man who inherited his father's store or farm." —C. Wright Mills

558. *Nolo contendre* (the Agnew family motto)

559. Peggy Noonan, for crafting the greeting-card sentiments that made Reagan and Bush sound almost human

560. The Newt-onian myth of the "Normal American"

561. Ollie North's gap-toothed smile

562. Nostalgia for the Cold War

563. Nostalgia for "Flesh-"colored Crayolas

564. Not all Republicans are billionaires, but all billionaires are Republicans.

565. Robert Novak

566. Cutting nutrition programs for the poor

567. In your heart, you know they're nuts.

568. They took secret solace in the O. J. verdict, because it proved once again that money can still keep a rich man out of jail.

569. Ocean dumping

570. Oklahoma

571. *Oklahoma!*

572. Old money

573. The 1 percent of American families who control 40 percent of American wealth

574. Operation Rescue

575. "I have opinions of my own—strong opinions—but I don't always agree with them." —George Bush

576. Option traders

577. Orange County, California

578. Orphanages

579. The Osmonds

580. They're willing to believe that there's a commie behind every bush but not that there's a hole in the ozone layer.

581. The pathetic gropings of Senator Bob Packwood (at least Democrats don't fool around when they're fooling around)

582. Palm Beach (especially now that the Kennedys have left)

583.  Palm Springs

584.  The pardon of Nixon by Ford

585.  The pardon of the Iran-Contra defendants by Bush

586.  Park Avenue

587.  The Buick Park Avenue

588.  They invented passive aggression.

589.  Reagan's firing of the Patco air-traffic controllers

590.  They blew the "Peace Dividend" on more weapons.

591. "Peacekeeper" missiles

592. Norman Vincent Peale

593. Pebble Beach

594. They just adore a penthouse view.

595. "Permanent replacement workers"

596. Ross Perot (he's a Republican whether he admits it or not)

597. Philanthropy based only on tax deductions

598. They're prone to phlebitis, a.k.a. Nixon-Quayle Syndrome, or the gout of the late Twentieth century ruling class.

599. Pinstripes

600. Plaid pants

601. Plaid golf pants

602. Plaid golf knickers

603. Planned obsolescence

604. One word: Plastics

605. They consistently include electric chairs, firing squads, gas chambers, hanging, lethal injection, and the Right to Life as planks in their party platforms.

606. Platinum credit cards

607. The White House Plumbers

608. They're more likely to have roots going back to Plymouth Rock than Ellis Island.

609. Polo

610. Polo shirts with crocodiles

611. Ralph Lauren's Polo

612. They know exactly how many polo ponies you have to own in order to qualify for a "farm" tax shelter.

613. Polyester

614. Pork barrel legislation

615. They get their pornography fix from *Baywatch* and the annual swimsuit issue of *Sports Illustrated*.

616. Mr. Potatoe-Head

617. Power breakfasts

618. Power lunches

☆ ☆ ☆ ☆ ☆ ☆ ☆ ☆ ☆ ☆ ☆ ☆ ☆ ☆ ☆ ☆ ☆ ☆ ☆ ☆ ☆ ☆

619. Power as an aphrodisiac

620. The Powers That Be

621. Precious Moments figurines

622. They prefer subdivisions to wetlands

623. Prep schools

624. Preppies

625. Loans below the prime

626. Prime rib

☆ ☆ ☆ ☆ ☆ ☆ ☆ ☆ ☆ ☆ ☆ ☆ ☆ ☆ ☆ ☆ ☆ ☆ ☆ ☆ ☆ ☆ ☆

627. Prime time

628. Private banking

629. Private aviation

630. Private beaches

631. Private enterprise

632. Private health insurance

633. They talk about the "private sector" as if it were the benign guardian of public wealth rather than a racket fixed for the rich by the rich.

634. Privet hedges

635. Processed "food"

636. They profess the ability to distinguish between Glenlivet and Cutty Sark.

637. Profiteers

638. They prefer property rights to civil rights

639. Proposition 2-1/2

640. Proposition 13

641. They insist upon imposing the Protestant Work Ethic on those who aren't.

642. They proudly display photos of their dogs.

643. They proudly display photos of their horses.

644. They proudly display photos of themselves with the Shah of Iran.

645. They believe that the only public housing worthy of federal funding is the kind that comes equipped with electrified fences and guard towers.

646. They believe that the only public sculptures worthy of federal funding are heroic depictions of dead warriors on horseback.

647. Puritanism

648. They define the pursuit of happiness as the pursuit of dollars.

649. They wouldn't think of going to bed without putting on pajamas.

650. Dan Quayle

651. "I have never been a quitter." —Nixon's resignation speech

652. The rabbit that attacked Jimmy Carter

653. Racquet Clubs (or any racket in which a *k* is replaced with a *qu* in order to justify charging exclusionary membership fees)

☆ ☆ ☆ ☆ ☆ ☆ ☆ ☆ ☆ ☆ ☆ ☆ ☆ ☆ ☆ ☆ ☆ ☆ ☆ ☆ ☆ ☆

654. The Radical Right

655. They don't care about the devastation of the rainforest because no medicinal plant grown there could possibly cure what ails them.

656. They want to raise the speed limit (they can afford new cars).

657. They think *Rambo* is a more realistic portrayal of Vietnam than *Platoon*.

658. Ayn Rand

659. Random drug testing

660. Random locker searches

☆☆☆☆☆☆☆☆☆☆☆☆☆☆☆☆☆☆☆☆☆☆

661. They would rather see you dead than red.

662. "Read my lips"

663. They canceled their subscriptions to *Reader's Digest* because of its nasty liberal bias.

664. Nancy Reagan's bulletproof hair

665. "A dope with fat ankles." —Reagan insider Frank Sinatra on Nancy Reagan

666. Ronald Reagan's jellybeans

667. Reaganomics

668. "Reagan Red"

669. Real estate speculators

670. Real Food for Real People

671. The only reason for treason that they can understand is greed.

672. Bebe Rebozo

673. They prefer recreational vehicles to recreational drug use.

674. Redistribution of wealth from the middle class to the truly wealthy

675. Redlining

676. The red peril

677. Red power ties

678. "If you've seen one redwood, you've seen them all."
—Ronald Reagan

679. Donna Reed

680. Ralph Reed and the Christian Coalition

681. They believe that the "boat people" were victims of a badly-run regatta.

☆☆☆☆☆☆☆☆☆☆☆☆☆☆☆☆☆☆☆☆☆☆☆

682. Regressive sales taxes

683. They relax on vacation by pulling brown leather sandals over black socks.

684. Remington bronzes of cowboys and Indians . . . now *that's* art

685. They've replaced the War on Poverty with the War on Puberty.

686. Reptiles

687. Resort fashions

688. Restaurants that require jackets and ties

689. Return to the rote recitation of the three "R's"

690. "Revenue enhancements" in lieu of taxes

691. When asked the most important Cuban of the 1950's, they are more likely to name Ricky Ricardo than Fidel Castro.

692. Riding mowers

693. The right side of the tracks

694. Right-to-Life as a euphemism for reproductive slavery

695. Right-to-work as a euphemism for union busting

696. The right to unfettered consumption

697. The New Right

698. The Old Right

699. "Rightsizing" corporate workforces

700. Right-wing dictators

701. They like the "rising tide" because they've got enough money to buy a boat.

702. They don't use the term "robber baron" anymore.

703. Pat Robertson

704. The delusion that Norman Rockwell is an artist

705. Knute Rockne

706. Rodeo Drive

707. They watch the Rodney King tape for entertainment.

708.

709. Rotarians

☆☆☆☆☆☆☆☆☆☆☆☆☆☆☆☆☆☆☆☆☆☆

710. ROTC

711. They believe the only safe sex is no sex at all.

712. Sailing

713. Sales

714. When being honored with a 21-gun salute, they instinctively aim it toward Moscow.

715. Salvadoran death squads

716. San Clemente, California

717. They prefer San Diego to San Francisco.

718. Savile Row

719. Neil Bush's Silverado S-and-L bailout

720. Scabs (or, "permanent replacement workers")

721. Phyllis Schlafly

722. School ties, the kind you wear around your neck

723. School ties, the kind where your frat brothers get you an entry-level job as the vice president of the local savings and loan

724. Marge Schott

725. Arnold Schwarzenegger

726. They buy second homes just when most people are still defaulting on their first.

727. They preach self-reliance, then vote bailouts for savings and loans.

728. They see selfishness as a virtue.

729. Self-righteousness

730. Tom Selleck

731. Separate and unequal

732. Their servants cringe when they're told they're "just like a member of the family."

733. *The 700 Club*

734. They construe the word "sex" from a cloud formation in *The Lion King*, then accuse the rest of us of having dirty minds.

735. Sexism

736. Shredded documents

737. The Silent Majority

738. Simple strands of pearls

739. Frank Sinatra, post-1980

740. Skinheads

741. Skull and Bones

742. The all-American "smiles" of beauty pageant contestants

743. They remember a time when belching smokestacks were a sign of industrial progress.

744. Social climbers

☆☆☆☆☆☆☆☆☆☆☆☆☆☆☆☆☆☆☆☆☆☆☆

745. The Social Register

746. Socialites

747. Phil Gramm's soft-porn portfolio

748. Soldiers of fortune

749. They prefer filet of sole to soul food.

750. "Some of my best friends are . . ."

751. They think that their sorority sisters actually like them.

752. *The Sound of Music*

☆☆☆☆☆☆☆☆☆☆☆☆☆☆☆☆☆☆☆☆☆☆☆

753. The sound of Sousaphones

754. Nixon's "Southern Strategy"

755. They consider women, minorities, children, the poor, and the elderly "special interests"; white men of business (who make up the other 10 percent of the population) are not.

756. The "special relationship" between Ronnie Reagan and Margaret Thatcher

757. Speciesism

758. They consider Arlen Specter a dangerous liberal.

☆☆☆☆☆☆☆☆☆☆☆☆☆☆☆☆☆☆☆☆☆☆☆

759. Spin doctors

760. Sport utility vehicles (whose primary utility lies in keeping the American gasoline refineries operating at full capacity)

761. Sports that require owning your own horse

762. Squares

763. Staffordshire dogs

764. Status symbols

765. The Status Quo

☆ ☆ ☆ ☆ ☆ ☆ ☆ ☆ ☆ ☆ ☆ ☆ ☆ ☆ ☆ ☆ ☆ ☆ ☆ ☆ ☆ ☆ ☆

766. George Steinbrenner

767. Stiff upper lips

768. The stock tables are the first section of the newspaper they read.

769. They advocate "stoicism," a.k.a. silence, among the poor.

770. Stretch limousines

771. They see more harm in strippers than strip mining.

772. Suburbia

☆☆☆☆☆☆☆☆☆☆☆☆☆☆☆☆☆☆☆☆☆☆

773. The Sun Belt

774. Supply siders

775. Survivalists

776. Talk radio

777. Tax breaks for millionaires

778. Tax-exempt mutual funds

779. Tax lawyers

780. Tax shelters

781. They use taxidermists instead of plastic surgeons.

782. They consider taxis public transportation.

783. Reagan's Teflon presidency

784. Televangelists

785. Telemarketers

786. TelePrompTers

787. They know how to "work" a telegenic war wound

788. Tennis

☆☆☆☆☆☆☆☆☆☆☆☆☆☆☆☆☆☆☆☆☆☆☆

789. Tennis "whites" that aren't clothes

790. Term Limits: an issue they ran on and promptly dropped as soon as a Republican majority was elected in '94

791. They believe testosterone conveys both intelligence and leadership ability.

792. They're as sound as a dollar.

793. They think cole slaw is soul food.

794. Clarence Thomas

795. They believe in a "Thousand Points of Light" and enough live-in help to turn them all on.

796. Three Mile Island

797. They laugh *at* the Three Stooges, not *with* them.

798. Strom Thurmond

799. Thurston Howell III

800. Men who wear ties without the explicit coercion of a written dress code

801. Tiffany's

☆ ☆ ☆ ☆ ☆ ☆ ☆ ☆ ☆ ☆ ☆ ☆ ☆ ☆ ☆ ☆ ☆ ☆ ☆ ☆ ☆

802. Tobacco lobbyists

803. Alvin and Heidi Toffler

804. *Town & Country* (the magazine)

805. Town and Country (the luxury Chrysler minivan)

806. The Traditional Values Coalition

807. They think that wearing a Jerry Garcia tie to their job at the bank makes them different from their fathers.

808. They want to transform the Internet from an anarchic freeway for hackers into yet another toll road for businesses.

809. Trench coats

810. Anything that "trickles down"

811. Trophy cars

812. Trophy homes

813. Trophy wives

814. Donald Trump

815. They trust big business more than big government.

816. Trust funds

817. They turned the L-word into  an epithet.

818. They own their own tuxedos.

819. Twin beds

820. Tycoons

821. Type-A personalities

822. The Ugly American

823. They understand (because they wrote) the secret racial code of real estate advertisements.

☆ ☆ ☆ ☆ ☆ ☆ ☆ ☆ ☆ ☆ ☆ ☆ ☆ ☆ ☆ ☆ ☆ ☆ ☆ ☆ ☆ ☆ ☆

824. Unemployment is their preferred method for bringing down inflation.

825. *Up With People*

826. The "upper crust" (or, the scum that bubbles to the top and congeals)

827. The Upper East Side

828. Their unhealthy interest in their employees' urine.

829. *USA Today*

830. Utah

☆ ☆ ☆ ☆ ☆ ☆ ☆ ☆ ☆ ☆ ☆ ☆ ☆ ☆ ☆ ☆ ☆ ☆ ☆ ☆ ☆ ☆ ☆

831. The V-chip

832. Valet parking

833. They only values they're really concerned about are property values.

834. If not for Amy Vanderbilt and Emily Post, they'd be forced to deal with other human beings in something other than a politely superficial way.

835. Velveeta

836. "Voodoo economics"

837. Vouchers for private and parochial schools

838. Non-counterfeit Louis Vuitton bags

839. Wall Street

840. **THE WALL STREET JOURNAL.**

© 1996 Dow Jones & Company, Inc. All Rights Reserved.

841. They rooted for Gordon Gecko in the movie *Wall Street.*

842. They want everyone to work hard so they don't have to.

843. *The Washington Times*

844. WASPs

845. "What a waste it is to lose one's mind—or not to have a mind. How true that is." —Dan Quayle addressing the United Negro College Fund in 1989

846. Watergate

847. Andrew Lloyd Weber musicals

848. Wedding receptions at which no one vomits

849. Welfare for aerospace companies

850. Welfare for automobile manufacturers

☆ ☆ ☆ ☆ ☆ ☆ ☆ ☆ ☆ ☆ ☆ ☆ ☆ ☆ ☆ ☆ ☆ ☆ ☆ ☆ ☆ ☆

851. Lawrence Welk

852. The well-respected man about town

853. White bread

854. White-collar criminals

855. Federal country clubs for white-collar criminals

856. White flight

857. White folk

858. White food

859. White shirts

860. White shoes

861. White shoes with golf spikes

862. The attempt to equate Whitewater with Watergate

863. Whittier, California

864. They will go to their graves calling airline attendants "stewardesses."

865. George Will

866. Bruce Willis

867. Pete Wilson's subtle lurch toward the right in preparation for the '96 primaries

868. The WIN button

869. Windfall profits

870. Winning friends and influencing people

871. Witch hunts

872. Women who abandon  not only their last names upon marriage, but also their first ("Hello, I'm Mrs. Pat Buchanan.")

☆☆☆☆☆☆☆☆☆☆☆☆☆☆☆☆☆☆☆☆☆☆☆

873. Women who don't sweat, but "glow"

874. Women, like Marabel Morgan, who believe that Saran Wrap can keep just about anything fresh

875. Women who prefer to be called "ladies"

876. Women who believe that Henry Kissinger was ever, even for one second, the world's sexiest, most eligible bachelor

877. Women with a strong affinity for ermines, sables, minks, and all other subspecies of weasel

878. Wonder bread

☆☆☆☆☆☆☆☆☆☆☆☆☆☆☆☆☆☆☆☆☆☆☆

879. "Wood"-paneled station wagons

880. "Wood"-paneled minvans

881. Workaholism

882. Workfare

883. They wouldn't think of making love on great-grandfather's Persian carpet.

884. Xenophobia

885. Yachting

886. Yalies

887. Yuppies

888. Because Frank Zappa said, "Republicans stand for raw, unbridled evil and greed and ignorance smothered in balloons and ribbons."